In These Latitudes

Ten Contemporary Poets

In These Latitudes
Ten Contemporary Poets

Edited by

Robert Bonazzi

San Antonio, Texas
2009

In These Latitudes: Ten Contemporary Poets © 2009 by Wings Press
Rights revert to individual authors upon publication.

Cover art: "Lighthouse" © 1997 by Andrea Belag.
Used by permission of the artist.

First Edition

ISBN-10: 0-916727-53-X
ISBN-13: 978-0-916727-53-6

Wings Press
627 E. Guenther
San Antonio, Texas 78210
Phone/fax: (210) 271-7805

On-line catalogue and ordering:
www.wingspress.com
All Wings Press titles are distributed to the trade by
Independent Publishers Group
www.ipgbook.com

This publication made possible in part by a generous grant
from the City of San Antonio, Department of Cultural Affairs.

Library of Congress Cataloging-in-Publication Data

In these latitudes : ten contemporary poets / edited by Robert Bonazzi. --
1st ed.
    p. cm.
  ISBN 978-0-916727-53-6 (alk. paper)
  1. American poetry--20th century. I. Bonazzi, Robert.
  PS615.I4942 2008
  811'.5408--dc22

                                    2008037642

Contents

Introduction

Robert Bonazzi

The initial impulse for this anthology's title stems from the fact that I had encountered the work of these poets while they were living in Texas (only two were actually born in the state) – thus a certain sense of our being together in these geographical latitudes, even though most of the poems are set in very different environments. But as the anthology began taking shape it became obvious that the poets who had made the cut were writing from a perspective of early to late middle age – that is, writing in these latitudes of mature experience. And while all had published accomplished poems, their work has been generally overlooked by the critical establishment – a common reality explored in my "Poetic Diversity" column for the *San Antonio Express-News,* which focuses on books of poems and translations, usually issued by university presses and independent imprints that continue to publish the most literary poetry at the national level.

While these aspects tend to connect the poets – along with the consistent quality of their poems – *In These Latitudes* spreads all over the map of poetry, including texts about China and Syria, about the east, west and Mexican coasts of North America, and about interior landscapes and cosmic speculations. These poets speak in a wide range of unique voices and styles, and the anthology includes such diverse genres as lyrics, narratives, meditations, political fragments, formalist verses, and a mythical epic. "Poetic Diversity" indeed.

It is a truism that we can better understand our own culture by living in a different one. For a keen observer that experience makes possible a double perspective and a more objective viewpoint. To a sensitive poet's awareness, this balanced vantage of perception beyond one's culture opens new horizons of insight, enhancing rather than ruling out emotional expression.

"If you're lucky," writes Nancy Kenney Connolly, "you encounter in young adulthood an experience that shatters the complacencies into a thousand transparencies through which you see. From then on, you live in and out of parallel realities." For Connolly, this encounter had been living in India, which translates into her poetry "as an embrace of paradox; and likewise of Keats' negative capability, his insight that great art arises from what he describes as being in uncertainty. To be this open, to reach for transcendent understanding, is a blessing of the muse."

For Tony Zurlo: "Teaching literature and composition at Hebei Teacher's University in China altered my view of life. I felt as if I had returned to a culture inherently my own, as if I'd originated in China during another time and in another life," he writes. "I felt spiritually at home with a culture that still revered the Tang poets, a people who still expressed pride in the wisdom of a 3000-year-old philosophy...In the end, this was a spiritual awakening." Zurlo's selected poems from Mind Dancing evoke this China, where "everything about life was pure spirit; sometimes soaring, sometimes wandering, but always shifting and twirling in evasive dance." Besides non-fiction works in print on varied cultures, Tony Zurlo also brings great variety to his published essays, stories and poems. Here the focus could seem limited, except "China is the/mind dancing," so the layering unfolds in subtle variations.

Emigrating from another country to North America represents this encounter in reverse. Born in Syria but educated at the University of Texas, Assef Al-Jundi reflects perceptively upon the Middle East and the States, while also translating the poems of his father, Ali Al-Jundi, from Arabic for U.S. literary journals. In his lightest poem in this anthology, his narrator asks: "When was the last time/peace broke out because of a poem?" These poems emerge from an entirely different sensibility – his views were first immersed in an Arab perspective. Thus, he experiences reality in the States through that aperture, even though he has mastery of the North American idiom and has lived most of his adult life in Texas. This double-perspective includes a wry humor, for he does not view the Middle East through the gauze of western media. He writes about it from experience, providing us with a deeper understanding of cultures we do not know.

Born in China, Wong Siu-yung's poetic "approach is very much influenced by the Chinese sensibility," including poems she translated into English for anthologies. In their poems we hear different tonal textures – different from everyone here and from each other – expressing unique voices in English. Wong Siu-yung writes: "One seeks the larger sense of spirituality in nature and things natural. I'm a Taoist at heart, Confucian in practice, and Buddhist in spirit, while also being a baptized Catholic. Go figure. The -ism of this all is a way of living, not an organized way to see the existence of a higher being." Niether Al-Jundi and Wong are translators by trade; nonetheless both have constructed literary bridges across languages, creating deeper levels of cross-cultural communication.

Marian Haddad, youngest of nine children of Syrian parents, was born in El Paso (all her siblings were born in Syria). One of the five important elements in her poetics is sound: "Speaking two languages fluently (English and Arabic) and one conversationally (Spanish), I have been raised with and immersed in the way words flow in and out of each other in three languages. Also, attending an Orthodox Christian Church since childhood, a fourth was added: Greek." Her father wrote poems in classical Arabic: "The sound was mesmerizing, how the long e's at the ends of lines were slow, repetitive and beautiful; how there was form and meter in his writing." Haddad's linguistic workshop has been enriched by traveling in the Middle East and growing up in a traditional Arabic household – one located on the Texas border with Mexico.

Del Marie Rogers writes: "There must be a level of emotion. If I don't think a poem is arresting, powerful, I shouldn't send it away from home. When I read the works of others, I'm not looking for a display of education, or even wisdom on its own, naked, or perfectly executed form, vivid description – though all of these are present in good poems. Beyond these, I'm searching for a thing close to magic, human communication at the deepest level. A poem must take me to a place of new awareness, engaging mind and emotion, both. For the poet, language is not only the means of discovery but the medium of communicating the found. Living alert, knowing these things, is a good way to live." Her poetry is rooted in "small events," of which she warns: "Be watchful." The poems honor nature without naming or capitalizing. Surrounded by trees: "One crow speaks from the relic woods." Rogers returns us to symbols in her spiritual inscape, where "great trees persist alone" and "Once you have come this close/the moon will always know you,/and ask impossible questions."

Laura Quinn Guidry's tragic experience did not occur in young adulthood but in her mid-forties, and she was forced to accept her loss in order to find a way to live. "After my son died, reading and writing lyric poetry helped me survive – to live on in an unsettled world whose strange beauty, in time, I was able to see and describe. I love the pleasures and power of language – its rhythms and sounds, its ability to comfort, disturb and connect. In the poetry I like best and try to write, the language is simple, images are vivid, and emotions intense yet understated. Writing about loss, I believe the poet's work is to be reticent, to say just enough, to let the images speak." Guidry's poems here constitute a closely knit sequence on the loss of her son, on the stages of grief that fit no predictable pattern, and about healing through poetry.

Dillon McKinsey does not flinch from the influences of Christianity and traditional poetry on his poetry – a formalist poet, he remains open to all forms, as the poetry journal he edits proves. He writes: "Poetry, for me, is a hand-cupped artesian flow from the very springs alluded to by Christ, that fill the Divine pool we call the soul. This is one of life's greatest paradoxes – a part of the Kingdom within. By Nature, the pool is fathomless and crystal clear. But when its liquid inspiration is surfaced and incarnated, both adulteration and glorification occur. The more studied, skilled, conscious, and spiritually-centered the alchemist-poet, the more potent and profound the poetry. Many things can shrink or occlude the pool; many can open her, and bring her deep riches, where the pen can be dipped and wondrous revelations put to the page."

H.C. Nash, perhaps the most idiosyncratic poet here, creates an slyly inventive expression of North American "anti-poetry" at the opposite pole from McKinsey's formalism. Nash writes: "My poems spring up pretty spontaneously (often just descriptively, or in syntactical scraps) – which is not to say that I don't spend a good deal of time reworking them. I never go anywhere without pen and paper and stimulating reading or art material, which is why I am constantly moving around thick file folders of rough, half-baked, and potentially exportable poems. Is it compulsive, all this jotting? No doubt." Nash has been "jotting" for fifty years; he is the oldest poet here. He points out: "Search for 'poetics' and you'll turn up more than three-million sites. Search for 'classical poetics' and you'll turn up almost 1.5 million. Search for 'modern poetics' and you'll turn up almost two million. It all adds up. The subject, in any case, would seem inexhaustible."

John Herndon expresses ". . . a need to know who I am and what I'm doing here has driven my work as a poet and a man. In my own eye, I am a walking bundle of contradictions. I'm a wandering adventurer, and a comfort-oriented homebody; there's no place I feel more at home than anyplace in the wild." He remains involved in grassroots politics and the eco-wars in Austin, since "This is where my compost is, and where I know the names of plants and animals." We should know the names of those silent plants and untranslatable animals who make our environment possible – they are witnesses, but if we do not listen, who will hear the universe? His long poem, "Laurel Ash Olmos (1917-1989)," took time and research, and the text goes deeply into nature by turning this herbalist grandmother into a tree – and so-called: Laurel, Ash, Olmos ("elms" in Spanish). Dying, her past flashes through consciousness twice, and then she experiences a mythic life review. "The voices come together when all dualism, duplicity and dialectic are resolved. She rises on the kharmic wheel and yet does not cross over to Nirvana, instead does 'work worth doing,/save all sentient beings,' and 'she does the work of the world tree' to 'hold heaven and earth together/and keep them apart.'" All this with an understanding that trees hold eco-systems together and that herbs exist also in a spiritual realm. His phrase "in these latitudes" in this complex poem gives us another reading of our series title.

These poets are perceiving mid-life experience through a highly polished lens, expressing what most of us feel in an intense, clarifying way – except that they find ways to express it. Nancy Kenney Connolly articulates one of the thematic ideas succinctly in the first poem of this anthology, writing that "We are/both lens and mirror of creation." Poetic sensibility provides the lens through which poets peer into reality and the poem becomes that reflection of creation.

Nancy Kenney Connolly

Nancy Kenney Connolly has authored four collections of poems: *I Take This World,* winner of the Main Street Rag Chapbook Contest; *The Color of Dust; 33 Shades of Green* (with paintings by Jeannine Sharkey); and *Second Wind,* the most recent. Connolly "fell in love with India" as a Fulbright Scholar en route to a Ph.D. at Tufts' Fletcher School of Law and Diplomacy. With her first husband, father of her three half-Indian children, she spent several years in India before the family resettled in the States. She taught at Michigan State, edited college texts at Scott Foresman, worked as a stockbroker and as non-profit administrator, eventually returning to academia as a research associate in the University of North Carolina's School of Medicine.

The Space Telescope's Song

Mustangs of interstellar plains
we gallop spacescapes unimagined
by the passing specks of carbon chemistry
who see light's spectral sweep
like the man who in a rainbow
beholds one shade alone – let's say pistachio –
while we can picture the entirety
for we screen microwaves, infrared and ultraviolet,
x-rays and gamma rays: We are
both lens and mirror of creation. O, tremble
at such radiance. Galaxies swirl
like snowflakes in a gale.
Vast and vaster nebulae of incandescent hydrogen,
nurseries of newborn stars,
death shrouds of supernovae
in which we paw the dust of fledgling elements.
Who can rove the reaches of this universe
and think god has declared himself
to any chosen molecules of carbon?
Hell flickers as the slimmest candle
beside furnaces of cosmic birth and dying.
Come, ride with us the winds of space
and sing the aching beauty. Sing!

Practicing

Hours stretch like the Sahara
as, day after day, you craft words,
strain to high C's, land triple axels –
rehearse, refine, rut in the brain –
a self-inflicted anguish

                    your dream

spectators indifferent
to the twenty thousand hours and more
of sweat and pain and trembling faith –
the building blocks of pyramids
that, from afar, appear to rise with ease

                    to one crowning *speck.*

How briskly an arena clears
the last tossed rose swept out
and where a mystic power just reigned, an empty
shell. An empty shell? Is all that practicing
for this performance hour? Or

                    for the team, the choir?

When did you know it is in practicing itself
that you enter the white villa, an oasis
of green groves and clarifying light
where, absorbed in pirouette or palette,
oblivious to ticking sand,

                    you become creation?

Un-Framed

On the cusp of waking, brown eye lingering
in dream, blue one blinking into dawn,

the still-life irises wilt – so easily one
is seduced by every passing caravan

    on the silk road of sensations.

Then comes the startled squint –
too late –

the shape of certainty has sprung.
What seemed enduring

    reels.

Now, irises take root in clouds, fire
flecks high fescue. A wave

washes out of Turner's *Fire at Sea.*
I stand knee-deep

    in a tumult of light.

Gifts

if you would pleasure me
color the sky
       transparent
scatter innocence
       in the wind
set the door
       ajar, let
a stranger in

if you would offer gifts
give me the pause
       between two thoughts
the moment in
       Monet's shimmering lines
when dragonflies
       rise
from lily pads

amaze me with un-
       anticipations
for no good reason

No Rest

Like a crayon corralled
inside straight lines
your soul chafes to kiss off
its black bow tie

and plunge freeform
into vermillion, hot
as mustard, raw as blood
roiling pools of passion

undulating lava flows
Dionysian sweat –
and yet
as Apollonian strictures loosen

you seek a floor
a ceiling, structure
as after Scriabin's fumaroles
clear clean strokes of Mozart

Monologue for a Massage

When I lie down
and bare my flesh to the master
I will follow my unruly soul from the room.

I will go
back to Aurangabad,
to an evening emerging like a bud.

Before nails
were driven through
the feet of music, long before

the fig tree
dropped its fruit. Then,
nothing had been attained. Then, cumin,

ginger, and clove
crossed swords in my throat.
I listened to murmurs seeping through

thatched roofs,
a jackal sulking in the jungle. I was
white with desire. I will go back, breathe again

saffron dust,
orbit that far nebula,
a honeybee sipping its first nectar.

Intimate Illusions

You could live for the fleeting exaltation:
                an orange peels
and radiance erupts, a tomato skin splits
and a truth slips through,
a mist of motes scatters and a sunbeam
sears your breast. Be molten in the moment
in your solitary hammock
swinging to the rhythm
of your privileged orgasm.

Or run through sea oats to the edge
                of the sand. Dare
join the waves as they flow in
from pregnant deep to cobalt swell.
Flounce abreast of white-feathered crests
flashing, peacock-proud, a milky mustache,
flinging shards of limpet and tentacle –
only to roll over, immersed in debris
of receding illusions, bride of a sea
embracing every errant tide.

Drifting

As the mind drifts
                    memories
flutter down from overhanging cottonwoods,
whirl in unexpected eddies
                            and roar
two thousand feet below in a Norwegian gorge
                hammering like fear against the ribs,
you halfway across a hallucination
of canyon walls – a swinging rope bridge –
now glancing down at an armada of regrets
                swamped by frothing rapids
                    and yet, somehow
you drift along, clinging to a raft of old rhythms
washing down from lofty stands of bristlecones and bracken –
            waves of peace
lapping currents of grief – the breath of a beloved ebbs
                as tadpoles and dragonflies emerge
and the pages turn, the river a book of origins,
            the word of god shimmering over rapids –
                and who thirsts at a waterfall,
or needs a rope?
                    The river is itself a bridge.

The Sense of Touch

The museum sign says: *TOUCH!*
This rock is older
than anything you'll ever
touch, older than the solar system,
              even than the sun.

I press my finger to the hole
and probe a shard of stellar lust,
potsherd of some chance conjunction
perhaps ten billion years ago.
              And not a whisker on it.

I press again. As if a doorbell.
Perhaps someone from Betelgeuse will come.
No. This unresponsive iron and iridium
is chill as whence it fell.
              I think of the millennia between us –

that endless rhapsody of rash proliferation,
one thing leading to another. Oh, Apple of My Eye,
beside this, Genesis is artless
and miracle the arc
              from callous rock to your shy inner thigh.

Reckonings

I

All green motion, the
aurora borealis,

like water reeds
yea-saying overhead –

all acquiescent grace, a coral
reef, crystal jellies glowing,

to-and-fro of clownfish,
tang, and puffer.

Someone stands in the park
pushing an empty swing.

II

Evenings
flickering like flames –

all bravura,
a mockingbird

in the acoustic architecture
of live oak arches.

You get only
so many Sundays –

for whom
do you vacuum the Venetian blinds?

Reclining Woman

Fernand Léger, 1922
Et alii. Et alii.

Promiscuous being!
You don't say no to any
museum. Doesn't your lumbar region
tire of this position? Clad,
oblivious to fad, in that
timeless milky skin. And
those overripe raspberries!
What are you waiting for?
Orchids? Bonbons? Champagne? Chains?
When you get proportioned
as an ornamental pear, or cubed –
three boobs protruding from an elbow –
you can't expect old gallantries or props.
Do I detect a mandolin, an odor of musk?
Spread your legs, get on with it just once.

The Pieta and the Fig

Like virgin love, the urgency
in the speaker's voice. He lingers
on a rain forest trail, telling of the strangler fig:
its tiny flowers grow within its fruit
dependent on a wasp
to bore inside and fertilize the blooms.
A dance of life and death, poor wasp.
She lays her eggs, then can't get out.

His audience of ecotourists awed,
the speaker squints one-eyed through binoculars:
"The hatchlings do, but see, if they get blitzed
by vandals armed with DDT, the cycle's over.
No wasp, no fig. With nature that's forever,
two for the price of one extinct, and each unique –
unlike the works of man, who can replace
whatever with another."

His beading temples glisten. He
has brought me to my knees. I shut my eyes
to see. Did the vandal who blitzed the *Pieta*
scar only a marble nose? Sculptors
still chisel and chip, *none*
Michelangelo. Once, after Alaric,
the record of man's soul
hung on the nibs of Irish monks.

We Need the Stars
to Withstand the Suffering

What times are these
When to speak of trees is almost a crime
For it is a kind of silence about injustice.

– Bertold Brecht

And what are trees, Bertold,
but power exercised: their sun-greed
sucks the smaller saplings dry
and leaves the rose bush gasping.

Since the beginning, the gold coin
of this cosmos has been violence –
equity only paper money,
often laundered, never clean. And yet, Bertold,

the greedy trees stand tall, offering
a careless generosity of shade
to half-eaten corpses.
Listen to the music of their leaves
as they drum the wild wind's saraband.
How sweet, the tartness of their harvest.
Gaze long enough at them
and calm takes root, then courage flowers.
This is the second wind.

Athenian Shadow Over the Potomac

*It is the gods' custom to bring low
all things of surpassing greatness.*

– Herodotus

A man of stature,
a crag above all others,
must have raised a fist against the turquoise tides
        surging the Aegean coast –
still focusing behind his laurelled brow
on proportioned columns, measured discourse,
the leafy days when civic virtues
walked the streets in sandals, when Socrates
revelled less in scripture
                than in questioning –
until reptilian fury drove the greedy seas to crush
like clamshells on the beach
that splendid interlude in Earth's spin,
                that city upon a hill
where once had prospered the unfettered mind.

Elegy

Finger the silk Isfahan, its
filigree of tendrils ripe
with pomegranates – it gleams,
an ode to your exquisite taste –
and the more you try
to bargain down the price, the more
the carpet beckons. Then
a petal blinks –
stroke away the apparition,

but look again, a leaf
is quivering like a lip, there is
a face. Beneath the sheen,
a face. Unlike
the merchant's jowly mask.
He calls for cups of tea.
Dare another glance
and there, between the fibers,
fingers thin as threads.

The Rapture is a Mushroom Cloud

White on white – the breath
brushing
the primal canvas,
light,
iridescent, translucent,
       a shiver –

then warthogs
trample
the laden vines,
a crown
of thorns crushes
       loaves and fishes –

and the bee-buzzed meadow
is kindling
for Rapture, moon
smoldering,
sun a crescent of itself –
       ash on ash, the breath.

About that Rose, Ms. Stein

Suppose a rose

by the veranda
of a plantation south of Atlanta or

Mombasa, on stage at *La Scala,*
or shaded by lacy Costa Rican coffee trees,
slowly unfolds

aglow
like fine *amontillado*
splashed by a dew of molten sun. No one
could summon voice
and only a gasp would testify

to what is in the eye
of the beholder – not
varieties of geography
but grace that is of a piece.
It's the Fibonacci structure
of eye and cell and molecule
and petal, the harmony we share
in the arithmetic of nature.

On Hearing Renée Fleming Sing
Richard Strauss' *Four Last Songs*

The day's tasks loaf on the sofa,
sipping Shiraz,
the high-noon gleam
of a life's minor medals
gathering dust
on the mind's gray mantel.

The urge to sweat another hill
dwindles
in a landscape scowling
at the heart's consuming quest
to cultivate like Whitman
Jefferson and Socrates
that flowering of spirit, that blossoming
of precious seeds – the rule of law
and equal rights and reason –
a reach and a fruition
once seemingly ordained,
but now
where can be found
among the husks, a harvest?

Light is loveliest at dusk –
in its consoling radiance
shadows slant at angles of repose,
a final fullness
hanging on the boughs.
The pear tree's white explosion.

Evensong at the Canyon de Chelly

They've gone now. From the canyon floor
the grazing longhorns, the backpackers
with their panoramic film, the blond laughter
that climbed a thousand feet of sheer red rock.

And from this mesa summit, the Navajo vendors
with their unsold turquoise and silver, grandmothers
squatting in specks of juniper shade, raven-haired tots
scampering too close to the edge of ancestral ledges.

We're here alone, my daughter and I, with purple
asters, a mountain bluebird. In sage-scented silence
we stand to watch a setting sun. Sapphire sky
and bleached-bone stone desolate in every direction –

what if our discord stilled like this?
Out of nowhere a stray bitch approaches, attaches
herself to us like a guardian spirit. Nose-bleed dry,
we spill our bottled water for the dog.

Assef Al-Jundi

Assef Al-Jundi was born in Syria and educated in the States. His poems have appeared in national anthologies, like *Inclined to Speak: Contemporary Arab American Poetry* (edited by Hayan Charara) *The Space Between Our Footsteps: Poems and Paintings from the Middle East* (edited by Naomi Shihab Nye); *Chance of a Ghost* (edited by Gloria Vando); and *Uncontained: Writers & Photographers in the Garden and the Margins* (edited by Jennifer Heath); as well as in Texas-based anthologies: *Between Heaven and Texas, Inheritance of Light, The Last Great Places in Texas* and *Poets of the Lake*. Al-Jundi has translated Arabic poems, including some by his father, Ali Al-Jundi, in *Sulphur River* and *Mizna*. Al-Jundi has an on-line page at www.myspace.com/lahab, where he regularly posts new poems and his experimental photographic and digital artwork.

Under the Sink

Science would have us believe
bears, bougainvilleas and butterflies
came into being
because of a big bang.

But what was ignited?
Who lit the fuse?

That substance which exploded
creating planets, moons and stars –
did it have kernels of life in it
imbued with dreams,
ready to emerge
as trees, frogs and water lilies?

Or did our eyes, lips and wits
sprout magically
from chemicals accidentally spilled
under the sink
of chaos' kitchen?

Blue Shadow

For my father

I

Thirty thousand feet above the ocean.
Wind and sand blow in cavernous spaces I carried
since our goodbye at the Castle Hotel.

I try tricking my mind
to make it to let go –

       Our morning coffees.
       These past few days in Larnaca.
       How we stretched them, bridging continents
       Fifteen years apart.

II

I close my eyes. Time is like air.
                   Damascus drifts in.

I'm sitting next to you at your favorite café.
       You think I am after the sweets you let me order
       like a grown-up.
       I'm there to listen to you talk.
       To watch you and your friends
       drink your coffee and beer.

You ask a palm reader to tell my future.
I extend an eager hand.
Imagine myself a grown man,
married, three children.

III

You,
insubordinate maverick
of women, wine, and poetry,
titled your new book *Sa'ara Rama' dun.*
Turned to Ashes.

I asked you
Does death frighten you?
You said
It used to.

You then stepped
into my faint blue shadow,
plucked shiny white feathers
from my wings,
and gave me
a handful of earth.

Pictures

As a child I resisted
standing in for family pictures.

No one could convince me,
show me how a *Click*
from an odd looking contraption
produced a photograph.

I took my first watch apart.
Wanted to find how
the *Tick Tick* is made.

What a marvelous little world.
Tiny toothed rings pulsing.

Much easier to take things apart
than to put them back together.

First question I remember asking my father –
What is God?

His answer was more puzzling than gratifying,
but after all these years
I have come to see
that even a donkey
has God in it.

Nomad

I'm up this cold night
You are still sleeping
But the birds don't know
to keep quiet

Something is calling me
More than your warm body
More than the touch of sleep
on tired eyes
Many times I'm beckoned
Or sent back
to open the eyes
move the body from under its covers
and converse
with spirit of the night

I often wonder where you are
when I'm up prowling
in this place we call home

Trance-position

You were here with me.
Worshipping with me.
Being worshipped.

When you turn off everything,
what do you find?

When you stand naked as a snow flake,
do you like falling?

Do you love your weightless body?
Can you feel me
devouring your name?

Perspective Adjustment

Condensed waves of force
pulse through my head
in heavy electric recitals

Twisted strands of muted light
blink off and on
across shuttered lids

Tight ropes of elastic menace
stretch from rear of the right eye
to base of my stiffened neck

Invisible bony hands grip and squeeze
with indifferent cruelty
fragile cartilages across my ribs

Fears dwell beneath control
Inborn vulnerabilities I wish
we did not inherit

Negotiations

We don't see eye to eye.
Our arguments leave us stranded.
Exhausted. We swear never
to speak again.

Standing by the living room window,
morning sun patting tired eyelids with warm fingers,
we thank yesterday
for picking up its old shoes and leaving.

Perhaps this new day can help us make sense
of how we walked through a door,
looked back and saw nothing but a mirror
on bare wall.

Situation

Despair or frustration?
Old question.
Logic of the world a lovely moon.
Darwin could be father of the universe.
Imagine his surprise!

Exit

How does one walk into a room without depth?
Make himself comfortable on a blue line?

How can one talk to his silent shadow?
Escape the noisy footsteps of others?

Pray
in one of your pockets hides a door.

The Night the Arab Came Out

Masqat, Oman

Was it the gentle night's air?
Spices and incense in the souq's alleyways?
Jagged peaks ringing the Old City?

The Arab came out beaming.
Soul in shoes.

My grief is an indigo ocean.

Holy Landers

Listen!
You are fighting over a land that can fit,
with wilderness to spare,
in the Panhandle of Texas.

You are building walls to segregate,
splitting wholes till little is left,
killing and dying for pieces of sky
in the same window.

The olive trees are dying
of embarrassment.
They have enough fruits
and pits for all of you.
All they want is for you to stop
uprooting them.
Sending your children to die
in their names.

Listen!
Your land is no holier than my backyard.
None of you is any more chosen
than the homeless veteran panhandling
with a *God Bless* cardboard sign
at the light of Mecca
and San Pedro.

Draw a borderline around the place.
Call it home for all the living,
all the dead,
all the tired exiles with its dust
gummed on their tongues.

There are no heroes left.

Collateral Savage

For Lebanon, 2006

Survivors of The Holocaust please
talk to me. Help me understand-
Do you sanction what's being done
in your names?

I thought your spirits
grew more gentle
having lived through the unspeakable.

Bombs are not less lethal or evil –
Stop being so deathly afraid
of the *other.*

A thousand eyes for an eye?
Children of The Holocaust
please do not lash out
as if you lost your sight.

Afterlife Show and Tell

You can bask in the glow
of the lovely Vishnu and Krishna.
Divine shine, indeed –
But here you have your own radiance going,
so what is the point?

Many choose
God of Abraham Retirement Community –
Sanitary clean. Gated, with serene angels flying about,
and fluffy white clouds in eternal blue sky.
All his prophets live here –
Still trying to outdo each other
with miracle reruns for the entertainment
of apathetic audiences.

Over there on a hillside is Buddha's temple.
He does not smile much any more.
(His attempts at losing himself futile.)
He has gotten chubbier.
He sits around moping all day.
No one comes to rub his belly any more.

Rumi sways down an alleyway
serenading a drowsy moon.
Inside a tavern
Hafez laughs, reading his poetry
in a circle of friends.

And in a nearby fragrant garden of lovers
worlds dance in and out of opulence.
Here music and wine
are themselves intoxicated.

You still want religion?
There,
see that donkey?
Go ride it
and ask it to take you home.

A Definition I Can Embrace

My wakefulness
can not wrap itself
around my spirit,
or grasp how a fish
hatches from a tiny egg,
or how a hummingbird
suspends itself in flight
to savor deep nectar.

In truth, my wakefulness is barely
able to stroke the fine-tuned ends
of its senses.

I do not understand the choices
others make, nor do I want to now.

If I am a seeker
trudging up a steep mountain,
what do I hope to find at the summit?
Myself, of course,
making peace . . .

Clutch

If I were alive before I was conceived
in a world without distances,
a time of countless
zones,

If that is home away from this baffling
space of straight lines,
universe of curved
light,

If forgetting is a necessary condition,
remembering an exception
of playful lunacy or
sudden illumination,

If translation
is an alluring
distortion
at best,

What chance do I have of ever hearing
more than a vague echo of my voice,
seeing but a faint apparition
of my being?

Old Hats

When you hear a poem read,
you may smile, nod approvingly,
break into gracious applause.
Or you may fidget behind a stoical face,
feeling the ribs of a stiff chair.

Perhaps you prefer to read a book?
Look at the poems stacked in their boxes
like ripe peaches.
Feel fuzzy skin, smell
warm nectar, pick
the juiciest.

The poem asks: *What am I for?*
When was the last time
peace broke out because of a poem?
Can a thousand poems save
one olive tree?

The poem can be a glum creature
when her grand ambitions come calling
dressed in extravagant old hats.
She leaves, seeking the acquaintance
of lesser, yet likely wiser, yens:
Salty olive with a fat pit
in the mouth of a refugee.
Wailing stone in clenched fingers
of a daring teenager.
And what the hell,
a ripe peach.

If the Planet Were Covered

If the planet were covered with wildflowers,
and someone dies a cruel death in China,
all the blooms would disappear.
A space of darkness would fill their place.
A time of sorrow.

Have you ever drunk from eternity's cup?
Eternity has never tasted so good.
Why would I wake up with a wildflower-
covered world, death in China, and eternity?
Only my dreaming-self knows!

All poetry is assembled from letters of an alphabet.
All these diverse faces are two eyes, two lips and a nose.
Everything we ever knew or will know
can be told with ones and zeros.
You still think creation is that complicated?

My heart is covered with wildflowers.
I think I will go back to sleep and grow some more.
This world could render me arid with blowing winds
if I did not drink and drink,

Pour thunderstorms of blue grief . . .

Title on Bottom Middle

Connect.
Plug into a mood.

Dare to give
solitude.

Grief?
Even a big blue ocean

blasts
thunderstorms.

Seeds

Some seeds,
lentils, chickpeas,
sprout the first chance they get.
Lay them on a piece of wet cotton,
newborn roots break out in days.
Brittle shoot,
tiny leaves
follow.

To hasten the birth of a mountain laurel,
thin its kernel's shell with a metal file.
Drop it in acid.
Anything to help water
infiltrate solid
crimson armor.
Left to its nature,
it seeks permanence –
A snug crevice in limestone.
Sheltered pocket under a fallen limb.
It waits for weather to show all its faces
before it begins yielding
to moisture.
More moons pass
before the old stone
cedes its heart.

I Am Earth

Under an oak tree
a world climbs at my toes

I find a purple door
step into your dream

A boy kicks a soccer ball
down a dusty street in an old city

A man slips across a border
between escape and refuge

A sage opens a window
in a candle-lit room

A million acorns
falling

Del Marie Rogers

Del Marie Rogers' 2002 book of poems, *She'll Never Want More Than This,* was a finalist for the Texas Institute of Letters poetry prize. Her work has been praised by poets Robert Bly and William Matthews. Rogers has authored three other poetry titles: *Close To Ground, Breaking Free* and *To the Earth;* her poems have appeared in many literary journals and anthologies. Born in Washington, D.C., she moved as a child with her family to Dallas. Rogers has lived in north Texas since 1975, except for two years in Taos, New Mexico.

True Dawn

Lovely colors flood upward, outward.
False dawn's the one on the wrong horizon;
easy, unless you have lost
all sense of direction.
Two halves of the sky's airy kingdom
compete, matched equals in beauty,
but one wing fails, falters.

One whole sunrise hovers westward,
soft as the fragile colors of thought,
rays drawn from an earth-dark center.
All colors are the grand illusions
of earth's blanket of dust.
Yet they can possess your hands, body –
there's hope enough to keep for life.

True dawn's obsessed with stubborn fact.
Probes corners to disrobe every lie.
When sun's sharp eye edges over
high rock, you can look only sidelong,
can't keep your footing, shaken,
or you'll stand stock-still as a plant to wait
for the slightest breeze.

Each day, raw belief in living things
that last the night. Or sudden loss,
washed corpse, animal dead in a storm,
bodies littered in a field of war.
Flat-bladed truth can stun you thoughtless.
Dawn brings desire to learn what is,
to live all day in love with that.

The Crow's Voice

There are small events. Be watchful.
The cat has a nightmare, deep-furred, twitching.
This is real: I hear wing-beats.
A moon, almost full, fog-haloed,
drops steeply through blackness.
No, we are falling, twisting
on a stone-buried axis.

One crow speaks from the relic woods.
After great silence, an eager whistling,
rich chorus of voices.
This also exists.
I could never imagine a thing so important.
Sounds of traffic rise, relentless,
close all night, rough breath of the city.

How I Live

A tall gray bird pauses, briefly,
on the iron rail fence between apartments –
nothing familiar, new shape, soft head,
elegant, an immature raptor.

The crows are shouting *leave or die.*
I do understand the bird will never
belong in this neighborhood of Sheena's
Dance Academy, its sign pink neon,

construction machines, the astonishing high-domed
Sufi school walled off from the danger:
the rest of us, awash in commerce.
It's true, some of us are ruthless.

Crows shout themselves almost hoarse.
The wild bird lifts from familiar ground,
a knot of trees they think they own,
its body soon pinched to nothing.

Great trees are a steady comfort. The crows
will stay with me as long as they can.

Haiku Angel

I

The haiku angel
doesn't care if winged beings
are prohibited.

She lands where she likes –
no one can incarcerate
angels for flying.

She goes anywhere
without need of a passport
in all the seasons.

II

Long-lived, the angel
knew skies before pollution
and threats of terror.

She knows our nature.
Serious, she's not without
a sense of humor.

She tells two stories,
of irreversible loss,
unquenchable hope.

Drought

Cicadas are ready, alien race.
Bide their time. Some nights they swell,
lost hive alert in every cell,
to one great hoarse and mindless voice,

weave long wild strands beyond all speech.
A ceiling fan's our welcome clamor
to keep heads free of warning murmur,
lets us rest beyond their reach.

Wild animals draw near the house.
No edible plant has gone to waste;
everything's bitten down to dust
under the sun's relentless drowse.

Slow and strong, we'll wait them out,
pray electricity won't fail,
ignore a faint and distant wail,
fight random fear and restless doubt.

Behind their chirr, stillness has grown.
Even the insects well may starve.
Earth cracks to make a common grave.
The great trees persist alone.

Those Others

The sky was drained, empty.
I had fearful dreams,
no hope of strong companions.
This house fell stark silent.

The dark pushed me so far inward
I knew nothing else, could sense those others
as a brush of wings, or shaken breath.
Somehow they pull down rain, by wishes.

Once, night branches brought stirring promise.
Everything changed, that waking.
Sun spread mildly on the floor;
speech began, a gentle wind.

Earth's dust is dearer, simple dust,
because they rise.
I flatten my palms against that ground,
alert in the rain that shudders down.

Near Fire

Old smoldering charcoal calls to bright, blond
pieces of kindling, says, come close, let me tell you,
you live only once.

A log becomes smaller, hovering, frail,
like an old person, a child
born into a new life of fire.

Red coals, big teeth of bark, become fuel
for burning the body, as if a man's blazing mouth
swallowed darkness, consumed each part of himself.

Even the hardwood log, iron, indestructible,
lets go of its outer layers, listens
and collapses to the center.

A tree withers as if in the glow of fine fury
it forgot what it wanted, flails like a baby's arm,
compacts knowledge to the weight of a star.

Horses in Heavy Snowfall

Blind, they must live through memory,
walking slowly, or stopped, stock-still,
in the wild truth of storm.

By memory's candle, horses shift forward,
steaming bodies, one glossy hoof
striking sparks in secret.

Hooves touch earth, four points,
and move through snows to come,
complete, intact, the way stones sleep.

Look behind winding cloths of the past.
Adventurer, you won't complain,
though even the cliffs can feel this cold.

Even death is a mountain of surprise,
changing dark shape. It's not final.
Live past that, behind closed eyes,

in the body's night.
Now the eyes of horses are bandaged
with snow, wind, winter silence.

When their eyes are unwrapped,
a winding stillness will end,
high gathering of shadow force.

Each animal, alone in the snowstorm,
was almost blotted from recollection.
Wild beauty burns to the future.

The Moon's Travel

The same moon searches the cold Himalayas
and the Guadalupes, looms on your shoulder.
You're chosen to track its passage.
This body of light may be close, tangled
in dense trees, or could nest on an iceberg,
far to the north of ships.

The only living thing,
it travels a thousand miles to discover
a circle of stones, placid grass in the center.
Swollen with earth's rosy dust,
the moon can see through rock,
becomes a weight for souls.

Leaving, it turns distant, abstract,
flies off like a coin.
Then comes back wild and sleepless.
Once you have come this close
the moon will always know you,
and asks impossible questions.

Luck

Just when you think you are lost,
the moon lifts your heart,
makes it expand skyward, soft,

reminds you of your self, your skin.
You're the person you've always been
since night first touched your feet,

even if you pretend
to be no one, try to forget:
lean pure light pulls at your life.

After this, roads will open at sunset,
great clouds will pile up
when you least expect to feel their wings.

You're at the core of an explosion of birds,
with the luck to wish for
the right things.

Now you'll have something to hold in a fist,
under your coat, behind your eyes,
even asleep, or under the earth.

Our Path

The mild influence of ordered planets
can't reach us now. The signal's blocked.
A siren screams, we can't hear our thoughts;
the sleepless moon can't do its work.

We're driven to madness by something else,
a roaring freeway, exhaust fumes, jackhammers,
stored, silent guided missiles,
men beheaded before our eyes.

With the hurtful sound of shattered windows
filling the streets, how can we feel
the planets' pull? Once we were guided
along a path we were born to walk.

The Book

These poems draw me close
as a velvet pillow, a wildcat's tooth.
Hold riveting news.
I've read them as the verdict
in my own trial.

Rich food. I can't get enough.
Wanting to make them last,
pages in a thin book,
easily consumed,
I touch them carefully, slowly.

Poet, your words keep me awake,
recalling fires, wounds.
They form clues for a path,
parts of a puzzle
we'll solve together, under ground.

Life Story

Passion alters the body's outlook.
Body moves, brain follows, harnessed,
learns from circumstance, force of surprise,
pulled stumbling through amazing country.
It's more than learning another world
outside your skin.

It's yours, paradise, but you don't know
you own the vast wilderness, every mile,
choosing each turn of the path as it comes,
difficult, tangled, or vine-covered, cool.
Once you grasp Eden, your feet are planted
on a road to lost beauty.

Insects tune up at twilight,
weave a hum of deep content.
The moon pulls at their bodies, wings.
Whey they're ready, they'll sing like spellbound birds.
If you come to believe you won't live forever,
you begin to live.

Waking

The brain dawns on its stem
like a little sun.
A clear edge of warmth, love,
erases haggard shadows.

Wakeful enough to hold frail threads of sound,
burdened with music,
you're one of those returning
from the soul's excursions.

Dreams, vivid, need you,
exhausted, stiff with trying to help
those others. Dark water subsides
under white light, wide sky.

You'll trace forms as startling
as a black tree in snow. High branches.
The lost sun flowers
like a brain on its stem.

Tony Zurlo

Tony Zurlo has published non-fiction books about Japan, China, Hong Kong, Vietnam, Syria, Algeria, Japanese Americans, and the U.S. Congress. His poetry, fiction and essays have been published in over 100 journals, magazines and anthologies. Zurlo has traveled extensively, beginning with the Peace Corps in Nigeria and ending after teaching literature and composition at Hebei Teacher's University in China. Tony and his wife, Chinese artist and educator Vivian Lu, live in Arlington, Texas, where he teaches college English.

The Mind Dancing

To love China is to love not
    the thing itself,
    but the idea of loving,
    and never knowing.

Lovers will be charred
    by the Dragon –
    ashes into dust,
    the yellow earth.

Born in turmoil and nurtured
    in mystery, China
    is the vapor trail
    of newborn stars.

China reveals itself
    to no one –
    China is the
    mind dancing.

Dao: The Elusive One

consumes scholars
in a fantasy of the mind,
convinced they can analyze
and split it like an atom,

attracts philosophers
like gravity, so confident
of taming and naming it
with systematic logic.

From sea to mountain top
ten thousand pilgrims gather
chanting mantras, burning weeds –
all seeking the Way in vain.

Scholars call the formless
and nameless "Dao," but like
cosmic dark matter, it fills the void
with the nothingness that is.

Dao: The Eternal One

Dawn shed her night clothes
and bathes in a snow-melt brook.
Blossoms perfume the air.

Buttered layers of sun
glaze fields with jellied primrose.
Sun sets, exhausted.

Frost paints meadows
with afterthoughts of summer.
Winter's sleep descends.

Lao Zi

"The name that can be named
is not the eternal name."

Lao Zi wasn't his real name.
Like the Dao he claimed no name
and every name.

"A hundred schools contended"
over the nature of human nature.
Good or bad?

Their battles destroyed careers
as sages debunked each others' views
as unnatural.

Every thinker in the land
had a theory, and every theory
had a name.

Except for Lao Zi's. He proposed
that naming was a disguise
for ignorance.

Lao Zi had little else to say,
so he bowed and retreated
to the mountains.

A guard asked for his passport.
Lao Zi asked for a brush, ink,
stone, and paper.

He sat on the ground and with
quick strokes he wrote out
       essential lyrics.

Leaving his poems with the guard,
Lao Zi disappeared through the pass
       forever.

For centuries now, they've studied
his passport for clues of his
       location.

They've probed the dense forests,
examined the pebbles in streams,
       but his trail

Has led to everywhere and to
nowhere, his destination
       unknown.

Village Pageant

Peasants bob like chickens
pecking at the stubborn ground.
A boy with bamboo arms beckons
a donkey and a reluctant hound.

Garments loiter all day
like ghosts with lethargic eyes.
Children tease each other at play
while elders comfort babies' cries.

Along a loess-dusted road a generation
of women stroll, each voice an instrument
from the past, each step a celebration
of an ageless Chinese village pageant.

Unbuilding Walls

In summer I arrived at the Great Wall,
confident that a pile of stones
alone could never block my path,
convinced my will would overcome.

So I circled circles and circled more,
wearing out ten thousand li of sand.
Each time I fell and glanced ahead
each grain grew ten meters tall.

Ten thousand grains of sand
I tossed that fall, and still the wall
stood firm through the first frost,
and many rocky cliffs still unclaimed.

I began to doubt and prepared for winter.
I gathered stones for my own fortification,
measuring each angle deliberately,
leveling and testing each layer.

I reinforced against the north wind
and erected a snow fence to the west.
Armed each morning I marched out
to inspect my private wall for breaks.

In the spring, the southern wall yielded to
peonies. Then roses invaded from the west.
Under attack from all corners of the Middle
Kingdom, I surrendered to an army of flowers.

Shadows on Beihai Lake

Behind scaffolds the Buddha sleeps,
while shadows glide across the water
parting lotus leaves in their paths,
struggling against the current,
wings fully extended, circling
like swans in *pas de deux,*
or the firebird in defiant dance.

Couples climb the Buddha hill,
hand in hand, armed with cameras.
But none know the brilliance
of nature's will to curl East
and West around the twirling sun.

Beneath the "Cloudy and Shady Bridge"
yin and yang converge.

The Visit

"Like refrigerator outside" –
Your words a melody of Chinese tones
accented with eyes that hesitate
a pivot away from flight.

"Like warm stove inside" –
A thought caught loitering half way
between my throat and lips,
tumbling out of rhythm, out of tune.

Before I ask, you offer apologies:
the person I expected was called away –
Nonsense syllables to divert me
from the poetry of your eyes.

From those I read deeply and reach out
to touch the soul that guides them,
eyes wide like "lotus leaves dancing
in the chaos" of "the white wave."

Such courage you show to even ask
"Should I visit?" And then your surprise:
a half-smile, but unspoken: "Do I dare?"
And the lotus leaves rehearse their next step.

Untamed Love

She enticed me with not promises
that we'd seize eternity,
no silence, no peace –

Defiance, insubordination,
hostilities with the gods was her offer
if I agreed –

a perilous love,
boldly dismissing those who enclosed us
in the cultural swill,

a soaring love
that only the insane dare ride
into the void of galaxies.

With untamed love our armament,
we stormed the membrane
of the universe.

Yín

rules the night
from the shadows
of memory.

her words the waves
of creation, her voice
nature's lyre.

Through pristine air
she glides
undetected,

cradling the mystery
to her
bosom.

The Souls of Ghosts

A cold, restless wind
rattled my windowpane,
and slipping into my room
was not you, but dreams of you
or rather the ghost of you
listening to gossipy ancestors.

Not the bold adventurer
who ignited my imagination,
the golden-hued muse
of earlier dreams
riding the restless wind
across the great wall of culture.

The ghost of you came
to shatter my dream
complaining of ten thousand
glass tongues condemning
our romance, still just a dream –
A tragedy with no heroine.

Beware my Asian princess:
Into your room one night
a ghost will enter, or rather
the Soul of a ghost will whisper:
"Cultures are but whims of dust.
The heart is the pulse of stars."

A Simple Conversation

I talk to you everyday –
a simple conversation
about roses and gardens
dandelions in grass

should we plant wild flowers
on the hill? run ivy up the stairs?
how to protect our China Doll
from winter's freeze?

a few words each day
flung into turbulent air
casual thoughts expressed
by nature's breath

I hold up half the sky
while waiting into the nighttime
of our lives, apart –
endless oceans apart

I marvel at our lives
and wonder about eternity
and supporting half of heaven –
will there be time for simple talk?

Ink Stains on My Desk

I retreated into my study
to read the latest from Xanadu.
Her words tumbled onto my desk,
staining the mahogany finish:
"Dear husband, I feel shame that I failed
to introduce you to my parents."

From across the ocean, she wrote:
"Sorry that this is a forbidden marriage.
I only introduced my 'yang-gui-zi dog'
to my relatives. My white skin, 'yang-gui-zi'
husband who I love so much
is an outsider in my land."

My words carefully drawn
from the ink stains on my desk:
"Your 'foreign devil' husband
raises his pitchfork in response.
It matters not what yellow people think
nor white nor black nor brown.

"What are colors but god's way
of displaying the wonders of the world.
Some days I'm a dazzling red, others
an overcast gray. What color are you
today? Green or yellow, striped or speckled,
you're the end of the rainbow for me."

Waiting

Once flushed peach blossoms wilt
ten thousand li from me.
Crows circle above.

Shivering in spring snow the fruit
rots on a distant hilltop
on gnarled limbs.

You race after the crescent moon
to hitch a ride across the sky,
but it disappears into the sea.

I chase the sun into mountains
for a glimpse of what shall be,
but it is swallowed by the sea.

And we wait at dawn and twilight
and beneath stars at midnight
from opposite ends of the universe.

Wong Siu-yung

Wong Siu-yung (a.k.a. Susanna Wong) directs the technology enhanced learning development and support at the University of Texas in Austin, where she has been on the adjunct faculty since 1998. She has been an invited speaker at symposia in Japan, France and the States. Besides being a pioneer in the field of desktop publishing (she has designed many handsome books and journals), she was a founding member of The Open Theatre in 1977. Born in Hong Kong, she arrived in Austin in 1973. She has "an intense love of classical Chinese poetry," and her poems and translations have appeared in *Pangea* and *Sniper Logic*.

A Falling Leaf Tells Autumn

A brief storm broke the summer heat.

        The moon was full but shy.

A small breeze touched my face

As I was searching for a glimpse

        wavering between limbs and leaves

           in front of the driveway.

I caught a brown leaf willowing in the air.

Final Sendoff

Ancestors bless your descendant
So he will reach the other shore safely . . .

One after another
They queue up
Kowtow three times
Wish you a safe crossing
And a quick return

Your face – still stubborn, but quiet

      eyes – open and inquiring

      nostrils – hollow and empty

      chest – rising and falling

      hands – damp and cool

      lips – sealed

                You know.

I whisper to your ear
        no strings, no worries
            just go.

Setting the Table
for Mid-Autumn Festival Feast

A pair of bamboo chopsticks on each of
The folded orange paper napkins
Set properly on the table.

> Tonight
> use blue see-through rice-pattern china,
> for the children, too.

In the middle of each setting
A soup bowl sits on a six-inch plate.

> Last night
> your father came into my dream
> asking me to join him soon.

> *Next night*
> *If he comes*
> *tell him you can't, not yet.*

Bone dish to the top right
Soup spoon on the bone dish.

> *He has to be patient,*
> *too much unfinished business.*

Copper-twisted basket scooper
Neatly placed next to bamboo chopsticks.

> Put the pot in the middle.

Woman Washing Clothes by the Stream at the Korean Border

Three donkey carts hauling tree trunks
Tread narrow mountain gaps single file.

Young couple cuddling in locked arms
Behind frosted branches.

Children bundled in thick cotton-padded jackets
Digging mud in ice.

A Woman stooping by the cracked frozen stream,
Beating her clothes with a stick.

Dry brown hills flanking her crouching posture,
Two huge concrete chimneys loom over her head.

Black columns shooting up the afternoon sky
Dusty gray blankets the village.

Factory whistle breaks her rhythmic beating.

"Ah," she sighs, "another fifty cents for my husband
And prosperity for the village."

Drowning

She stared into the snow
As the soot from the afternoon fire set in.

She refused to feel crippled
Dreaded the need to warm the hut,
And to eat, and to drink.

To drink!
She had no liquor for relief.
She lit the last matchstick
Watched the flickering tongue
Lick trapped oxygen in the empty bottle.
But the spirit gripped her hardened nerves
And cramped her muddy hands.
She needed to get out of here
Before she drowned herself.

A bicycle skidded across the frozen dirt road.

A Snapshot

White mountains reflect green pine.

Sheets of clouds,

    Drifting powder,

        Quicksilver on the ground,

            Sparrows bathe in snow.

Travelers by the fireplace looking out.

On the Way to Work

Sunlight cascading through

    Mist rising from the stream

Frosted branches shimmering above

    Wire fences lined with dewdrops

Icy water rushes under bridges

    Along the winding ranch road

I dip my toe in the limestone water at Crossing 11

Wasabi Fun

White sun glides across tall windowpanes.

Silver threads web between leaves.

Glowing hearts slip into the magic of spilled art –

      a shape . . . an eye . . .

                        O My!

       a dolphin . . . and a heart.

Warm sake lingers in night air bursting with neon lights.

A Magical Moment

Clouds gather, rain drizzles, water pearls drop.

Framed by the windshield
egrets hop in and out of green pasture.

A trace of red wine, warm breaths and the sound of Tennyson
fill the air.

One glance locks the heart.

A sigh, a giggle, a burst of laughter –

echoes of the sparks in two little people

without suspicion.

Entering Spring

Late-morning gift of irises,

In buds with ready exuberance,

Burst in iridescent blue.

Handpicked, rare tea

    Steep in a boil of folded shells.

    Green leaves unroll,

        Needle by needle, stringing

           White blooms open.

I sit at the corner of the patio . . .

A flight of small birds cruises overhead.

A hummingbird thrusts into the hibiscus.

A fragrance passes my throat.

H.C. Nash

H.C. Nash has published a sequence of 101 poems, *The Poor Bastard Cycle*, and a book about Penn Jones, Jr., a first-generation critic of the *Warren Report*, entitled *Citizen's Arrest*. He has written op-ed columns for newspapers and currently writes his "Heads-Up" newsletter, highlighting connections between the political assassinations of the 1960s and the so-called war on terror. In 1968 he began a one-man weekday picket of the Federal Building, housing FBI offices, in Norfolk, Virginia. Over a nine-month period he gathered signatures petitioning for a new investigation of the conspiracy that killed John F. Kennedy, sending them to Rep. Thomas N. Downing of Virginia. Downing in 1975 co-sponsored the first of seven resolutions that culminated in a new probe of the assassinations of JFK and Dr. Martin Luther King, Jr.

The Evolution of the Mind

the evolution of mind
on Monday.

Mary had these
round wrists,

which in the bare birches
counted for something.

in the inner suburbs
we might have fallen helplessly

onto the giant surfaces
of exhaustion, ennui,

pathos, dreams,
sex lives, broken plates.

the groundhog hid out
under sheds, keeping all knowledge

where it is most useful:
in abeyance.

i do the same now;
i too hide out,

spooked by bathos,
spooked by claws,
waiting for signs.

the evolution of mind
on Monday.

Looking For

surveys tell us we spend
two years of our lives looking for
lost objects.
in the local case
umbrellas seem to hold the stage
most dramatically – misplaced always
just in time for rainy days.
keys?
the Central Repository for Lost Keys
brims over with such finds
at an otherwise bereft former Air Force base
in Mississippi.
& here we have Carlyle

losing his clothes –
"nothing beautiful"

i myself knew a woman
who has spent at least twice two years
looking for love,
not counting time
over her head in sleep
when dreams are prone
to join the search.
i myself have lost hooks & crooks
& in each case
forgot them all
before they turned up
again,

useless
in my
new life

An Admonition
Regarding Fact vs. Opinion

for every man's & woman's god's sake,
teach children early on the difference between
coniferous & deciduous trees,
tuna & dolphin,
those who have some faith in man
& those who have faith only in profit.

early on teach children also the difference between
fact & opinion,
so that when the lover sez to his beloved,

"you believe you have flaws & imperfections,
but you're a national treasure to me,
& that's a fact,"

the children will understand from that crucial point
that the lover in question spoke correctly,
unimpeachably,
without fear of contradiction at some later date
by logicians, historians, epistemologists,
& other specialists. that way
the children in question will speak in defense
(at least most of the time)
of the facthood of human hearts
the while they beat, the while they sing,
the while they stay,
& not a moment less.

God Still Hides; Man Will Search

God still hides; man will search.
if God does not reside in the Gaza strip
at least in disguise,
where might He be?

God still hides; man will search.
if God does not visit Earth
at least to wonder at oceans' scope,
what is preventing Him?

God still hides; man will search.
if God has never asked questions
about the questions of Pascal,
how shall He then be thought a teacher?

God still hides; man will search.
if God doesn't walk the rain forests of Brazil
or canvas occasionally the population of Asunción,
what good is He to liberation theology?

God still hides; man will search.
if God hasn't bathed in the Ganges lately,
what can be said of His empathy for
Hindi hygiene?

God still hides; man will search.
if God refuses to check on the sparrows
devastated by PCP's on the fertile plains,
what can be said of His early education?

God still hides; man will search.
if He failed to confront Stalin
when he had the opportunity,
what can be said of His sense of timing?

God still hides –
does this suggest He is more playful
than even the best comedians
among his creatures?

God still hides; man will search.
if His universe continues to expand –
providing more & more hiding places –
could He truly wish to be found?

God still hides.
man puts aside his searching ways
just long enough to purge the world
of false gods on every hand.

first things first,
but God still hides.
& man will search.

Some Applications of Willfulness

one can only imagine.
poor words themselves lean to panic
given such height, thrust, vista,
the ego monumental.
men, women, institutions –
old & new horizons,
brilliant matter of fact of
irresistible force, immovable blahblahblah . . .

below (generations below),
grid(s) of Manhattan histories, rock bottoms,
bottom lines,
Hudson valley, East River, United Nations,
bridges to sing by, Jersey, pure promise
& drive.
all hell had not broken loose,
definitions had not yet out-
grown themselves.
down from Boston

in tubes of the horrific
in rarified air
vectors, venom, vanishing acts
of worlds & oysters
& faiths met

faiths met there but did not speak.
flaming transparency of
pure dialectic:

nitrogen of great wings,
figurines of cell phones.
sacrifice in all seam-
less-
ness.

there was no vote on it,
nothing to be retrieved from restrooms.
(everybody on board knew that this

could never happen)

Suspension Poem

alliterations
of azure,

peace as meadows of
blueblack bulls.

A to Z ennui.

you can't even get there
from here.
in any case,
no one has asked.

water for the
treading
(our heads wouldn't
   consider swimming.)

the passive voice
finally
overcoming.

patience in pure pastel.
phoenix at intermission.
the most earnest lover
registering
absolute zero.

As to the Straight Line

as to the straight line,
as to the pair of points associated with it –

as to this meticulous plan to get from A to B
via this straight line –

as to the waste of effort
associated with any deviance –

as to the horizontal plane,
as to the azimuth –

as to our optic nerves & their reliability,
as to the clarity & economy of the concept –

as to the phrase *shortest distance,*
as to the axiom itself –

as to our plans, meticulous or nonexistent,
as to the motives inherent in our journey –

as to the curvature of the Earth,
as to the time of day & missing water bottles –

as to yr mood, mine, the governor's, the custodian's
the ethics of the surveying team –

a straight line is the shortest distance between two points.

now *move* . . .

Untitled but for Negatives

The fish that wouldn't bite
The door that wouldn't lock

The strings that wouldn't vibrate
The treasure that wouldn't be hidden

The waitress who wouldn't take a tip
The wrench that wouldn't grip

The turtle that wouldn't cross the highway
The child who wouldn't cry

Marian Haddad

Marian Haddad's book of poems, *Somewhere between Mexico and a River Called Home*, now in a third printing, received excellent reviews. *Saturn Falling Down*, a chapbook of poems, was published at the request of Texas Public Radio, in correlation with its poetry workshops. As an MFA and manuscript consultant, Haddad has worked with award-winning poets and writers; often judging writing contests nationally. Her lectures and readings have taken her to Tufts University, Hunter College, and to meetings of the American Arab Anti-Discrimination Committee in Washington, D.C. She has taught creative writing at Our Lady of the Lake University and Northwest Vista College, as well as literature at St. Mary's University.

In a San Diego Courtyard

This dark evening,
early December light still
surrounds me

– false light – real light – what is light?

I should be cold here, but I'm not.
Winter bypasses the Pacific. I sit

by this fountain,
water folding over itself
          and back;

water has softened the edges it skirts.
Persistence drives a stone mad.

Softening the edges.

The way the world would be
if only we let the water
     roll   over the edges
and back.

Watching the World from a Corner Table

I am the dark shadow
that is unbent – unable
to bend – somehow –
I arrive at this
humility, this re-routing
of space, as it were –

I am the dark
itself – it doesn't matter
what matter is
today – it only feels
to matter – it only feels
to feel this
unbecoming
day –
day in which
I did not become
any thing

What is this color here?
Here, under this beam
of light – it is the shadow
of a shadow –
The wall is here –
by me – I know this –
I touch it
 – There is no faith
that needs to explain
this (reality)

Today is dark again,
though the sun is still
here – half-hidden
behind clouds – I
came out in it today –
then lost it
behind the white
and cold grey air

Is air white
or grey?
Is air?

I am always observing things –
I've been told, "You have a wandering eye."

I see the colors of roofs
I see the sign
no one else sees –
people rushing by
without looking

Time

I'll tell you what – we are almost
run over by time – a Faulknerian
thing, perhaps. The ticking
does not stop. Away, away

the hours chime. And *us,* running
frenzied about, as if   we can beat
the clock. But when we stop, somehow,
to rest – or when the head

no longer aches – words – again.
It always happens like this.
They save themselves up
during the busy days –

When we make ourselves sit
by the waters of a river,
by the floating –
water sliding down –

When we sit awhile
in this constant place
of beginning – the night entering
its expected hour –

It is then – here – that the words
make their way out.   Here
they unfold. When the mind is quiet,
and the river   is not.

At the River

Gruene, Texas

I came here because
I know this place – because
I have been here before,
and I know where the river
ends – I sit by the part
where it foams
white above rocks – three
stumps reach far down into this
river – and there, across
from me, one seems to be
growing right out of cliff,
right out of rock. It leans –
graceful sway of trunk – it has
somehow found its leaning
comfortable, a sideways growing –
if something stays bent
long enough – it assumes its place
gracefully – learns to live
with that

Accidental Resting

I would never have planned
an hour by a fountain

spiced cider – the air not warm –
not cold

me – the water – rocks
around me –
a slow night

I'm supposed to entertain
the crowd tonight

but for now – I sit, almost
meditating

almost   not guilty

Driving from El Paso to San Antonio

There's a sad part
of the afternoon.

I love the first
light – and the whiteness
of the desert then.

And I love
the high noon
hour – and the sun
that beams.

Intensity
and becoming.
Even the few
hours after that
are livable.

I am in the stream
of the given day,
somewhere-in-between
between.

But then
it comes –
the hour
after that –
before the darkness –
the end of day –
the end of light –

It says something
about
the sadness
of endings.
Things that leave us,
the lost beginning.

And when that yellow
hue has trailed
its final sad note –
there is still
light –

a post-light
not yet sunset –
light outside
light – sadness
past – and me
in the middle
of that short hour.

And now
in my rearview,
a strong white sheath
spreads itself out
across this sky
– white again –
no sadness here.

I ride alongside
a semi –
following the same
blue sky
that leads us
shortly
into night.

This cool
evening –
and the windmills
blow – just past
Monahans.

The sun
behind me –
easting its orange,
its lavender light.

And I await
the evening
sky –
coming closer
to home.

Crack Cocaine
and Other Addictions

Your head at my breast – dark bird that comes to rest
against its mother's down. It's there you lay your cobalt fear.

I heard your mournful, quiet song in me resound
till my head broke with your silent plea.

Your heave of breath spoke sounds, not for the ear,
but for this dry and dye-cast bone in me.

And I sang you in mirrors, and I sang you in cars,
how the body takes in what it needs to drink,

and you drew, from my blue-black hair, the scent
that took the place of seeds. You breathed it in, this

instead of the white-powdered line, this scent from which
you took, or tried to take, the strength to face your fears

that night; and now, today, the way this rock, this crystal,
falsifies and splays your strength. I must not weep

as you crawl bent, belly-flat upon the floor.
Is this the thirsty hole in which you creep?

And now, your clear window is dark without your face.
A man stands by your banker's desk and chair.

He opens and shuts your door without your grace,
and light goes out quicker there. It was me

who stood alone behind your wing and gazed
at what was once a sturdy feathered limb, but now it droops

a crooked slant. I grazed the outer part of you,
the one I could not keep; it is this fear inside, the black

that will not sleep. It's this I lift up, like wood for burning,
before I move to lay it back into its dry and naked space.

I recall the touch and quake of you, the supple skin,
the blue soft vein beneath your flesh was all.

The inner arm I used to play like wind
plays itself on wheat. And there, the slow stroke

up and down your flesh, the inner skin. I traced it there,
like blue night sky before sky broke,

played it in time to the water's rock and wave.
It's there I stood against you, bare with brine and sand,

when moon ticked slow and voices sang. And now, I wait
for night's quick dreams to prick you clear, awake,

to think of me, perhaps, and know that I am silenced
by silence, cold and blue, you gave; I did not see

how great gaps could grow, the disassemblage of words
not minced, until I could not speak

but only quake. To know you were low
and I could not reach. I could only watch the way things break.

On Tulips

A dozen red lead sinkers around my neck.

– Sylvia Plath

Sylvia, how you were frightened,
scared, little child,
of these blossoms someone sent
to your white-washed
room. Washed up
and put out. Sylvia,
these tulips, like monsters,
are bleeding. They were always bleeding
down the walls of your white room.

Did you envy their color?
The way they stood up –
long-necked, bending slightly
sideward, like the necks of ballerinas.
Where you ever a ballerina,
you graceful child? Perhaps
you danced under your eastern moon
until something broke.

You are closer to your death here.
I do not feel your anger seething.
I do not see you joyful at bleeding.
You are tired, ensconced
in colorless resignation.
It seems here
you have submitted
to numbness, your desired
state. I am afraid to read you

for fear of breaking. How we
all might break. I put you down
carefully, so as not to frighten.
But here, between your tulips
and your white fluffed pillow,
you peek out from behind
your starched hospital sheet
at these blood-red flowers,
the color of living.

Words Apart

My brothers
do not know me.

They hear me speak,
but they
do not know me.

Their eyes are fixed
for a moment
on these lips of mine

that mime words
across a table, amid

silverware clattering
and conversation
floating above us.

Our blood
is the same color.

Embryos planted
in the same belly,

shot into
living

by the name
of the same man.

We sprang
from one mother's
womb, slid through

one dark channel,
suckled the same
sweet nipple. Yet

my brothers
do not know me.

Strangers who wear
my name. Worlds
apart.

I think I will die
someone who mimed words

across a table,
silverware clattering
in a busy kitchen,

or in a restaurant
at a table
with other strangers.

I Am Walking Back

to the bubbling center
of this river –
I cannot drop my pen –
I walk while I write.
This is how I pray.

Laura Quinn Guidry

Laura Quinn Guidry began writing poetry after the death of her son, and published her first poem at age 52. Her poetry has been published in several anthologies and literary magazines since. Born in Baton Rouge, Louisiana, Guidry grew up in New Orleans. She has called Texas home since 1980, currently residing in Houston and Carmine, Texas.

At My Window

Tomorrow it will be nine years.
Last night, the same sky
as on the night he died
extravagant with stars.
Then, the sun's return.

Today at my window I watch
a swarm of gnats flit in,
back out, back in again,
but never through a shaft of light
that could enfold them.

These gnats.
A frenzy of desire and fear –
suspended. Now they rush.
Now they are fire.

Covers

What mother hasn't stood over her sleeping
child to see if he is breathing?
He is so still and quiet.
The slightest movement of his covers,
a barely perceptible rise and fall,
relieves her fear and makes her feel
a little crazy.

I stood over my grown son's bed
when we found him,
so still, so quiet.
They were telling me he died in his sleep.
He never woke up,
never knew what happened.
He did not feel pain,
did not know fear.

I knew it was true
because of his covers –
the way they lay across his back.
He had not moved them.
He was still tucked in.
I felt the slightest relief.
I felt a little less crazy.

Things Left

Little things left half-done.
Bills sealed, unstamped.
Pizza hardening in a cardboard box.

The stack of cards to send
his fiancée week by week
telling her he missed her.

A message from the video store
said two movies were overdue,
late charges accruing daily.

We called to say he had died.
We rummaged around, found
the movies – I can't believe

I can't remember the names
of those movies. The young man
at the counter said, no charge.

In Lieu Of

When my mother died
her obituary read, In lieu of flowers
please give to the Cancer Society.

When my father died
our family said, In lieu of flowers
kindly contribute to his church.

When my son died
nothing was said about flowers.
I might have said

let the room be filled with flowers.
Let them overflow baskets and bowls.
Stand the sprays three and four deep.

Keep them coming.
Let people say they've never seen
so many beautiful flowers.

Let them cascade down his coffin.
Lay them high upon the entered earth.
Bring some home.

Let their sweetness pervade the house.
Let my senses be steeped in them
until they overbear me.

Angel Story

Don't talk to me of angels guarding
their earthly charges –
how they swoop down to intercept
Destiny, how their great wings enfold
the chosen and whisk them to safety.

Angel stories are all the rage now.
I'll tell another, about the one
who hovered above the bed where
my child slept and, this time, to placate
Fate, folded his wings and walked away.

Graveside

The clothes we chose for you –
the jacket you bought for your first real job,
the tie that brought out the green of your eyes
no one will see – I know are there.
But I can think you've gone on
to more important things.

Into the vast, still noon,
a sudden, unadorned truth
I can hardly think.

Everything that I will do
or will happen to me
for the rest of my life
will be with you there
and me here
against earth and stone.

New Grass

The grass has greened up.
September now, not yet cold.
Today clouds dull the sun
and a little rain has fallen.

In the hole where
the vase waited,
it is dark and brown.
Dried grass, shell of a beetle.

A spider on its side
legs crumpled like the wilted
petals of mums.
I fill the vase again.

At his grave, the scent
of grass, newly mowed.

Alone

Toward evening I travel
past ranches and small farms.
Alone in a field, a cow
eats the scant grass. Behind her,
dense trees curve away.

You know how it is when
just as you pass something
it catches your eye
and, then, in your mind's eye
you see it again?

It was as if all loneliness
lived in that one unremarkable cow
in her little field
her head lowered and night
already in the trees.

Old Song

A song on the radio,
an old, dreamy-sweet song,
serenades the girl I was.

Tonight in words and melody
the woman I am
grieves for that girl

who sang along with the radio
whose dreams were sweet
and all happy possibility.

Love Poem

My husband is driving
his tractor on the side of the hill.
Only his head and shoulders are visible,

his wide-brimmed hat.
He is fifty-four
and the sun has become unfriendly.

He cuts the wheel sharply.
The tractor bumps along the ridge.
He is the boy

in the photograph on the bookshelf
standing tall
on the pedals of his bike.

My husband disappears
down the hill.
The boy pumps the pedals hard.

A Few Words

I must learn to love this place again.
Once, I loved its distance from the city,
its bordering on wildness,
the way the old roses tangle and spill over stones.
I loved the laden silences and night noise,
nights so dark the farthest stars reveal their fire.

But when the coyote boldly
appears in our yard at dusk and dawn
and when, a few feet
from the front porch, the copperhead
sinks its fangs into the neck of our spaniel,
everything changes.

I must learn to love the world again.
The hard, unbounded world.
I have only a few words and some images.
Yesterday, the dog that bolted from its yard
to charge a car, and was struck.
Its strange gyration of adrenalin, pain, and bewilderment.

I want to blot out that image
and others. Still, I summon them.

Mourning Song

Sorrow sings to me in the morning,
a voice clear and lyrical.
Sometimes I hear.
Sometimes I'm off chasing an elusive
strain of night music.
The song seduces, then fades.
Mute and aloof, as death at dawn.

Without

I wake to the cadence of breathing
then remember
I am alone in the house.
The man, the dog, elsewhere.

I rise, my thin courage a wavering
flame I follow into darkness
then discover
the sound comes from without.

Hidden in a tree, an insect
vibrates and mimics
the rhythm of the breath in sleep.
Now, a shrill surrogate.

This Time

If I could reclaim a moment
the clean slate of a moment
a taut, white canvas
an anticipating page,
this time
I'd commit no sin of omission.
This time
I'd withhold nothing.
No lessons to be learned.
I'd live the moment
gratefully,
then give it back.
My prodigal,
pleasurable
moment.

Dillon McKinsey

Dillon McKinsey has been co-hosting *Writing on the Air*, a radio program on KOOP Radio, 91.7 FM, for several years. He is the past editor of the Monthly Bulletin of the Poetry Society of Texas and editor of *Ardent*, a poetry journal in Austin; he served three terms as president of the Austin Poetry Society. Born in Chicago, he was raised on a large ranch in North Dakota. He earned an MA in public administration and a second MA in clinical psychology. While living in the Los Angeles area for 17 years, he had a clinical practice in Pasadena. He has given over 6,000 lectures in 15 countries, lecturing on drug abuse, dream work and spiritual growth and healing.

Assumption

Words warm and evaporate.
Only the poetry of Being remains.
The primal, ashless fire –
The light that darkness envies,
Fears, and longs to be;
The ceaseless moment, all-in-all;
The timeless, sumptuous, inward call.

Cosmology

The world moves large and small –
Crickets chirp and butterflies flutter
In chaotic quakes and grumbling storms.
And I, as a child, used to watch the ants
And wonder at the earth of the worm.

Now six feet tall, the ground is distant,
And I must kneel to see.
Yet now, when I look at the ant and worm,
I seldom catch sight of me.

But the stars are nearer and clearer at night
With light from the edges of time,
And sometimes when my heart sits still,
I hear comets and crickets still rhyme.

Cattails

In fall
The cattails on the marshland
Weave the softness of their rigid forms
Like shuttles in the loom;
And I'm reminded of the patterns
Love creates in life –
The maze of an inner room.
On whited wings the senseless seeds
From cattails blow away,
While a breeze,
Impassioned by their fall,
In the rushes comes to play.
Oh, how the marshland reels in love,
As cattails take their stands –
As we are moved –
In empathy's soft hands.
So come into the marshland
Where the cattails seek the sky –
Where they explode –
Their seeds unload –
And in sweet pleasure die!

Humus Haiku

As brown leaves death dance
And bare limbs uphold the sky
Hopeful humus springs.

Necessary Losses

No song to sing
A birdless wing –
A leaf –
Falls down to brown.
Yet in the earth
Decaying mirth
Will fill the tree with sound.

Fear of Flying

Backwards,
Toward the nervous western coast
I take the *jaqui* way on tin foil wings
Against the morning turquoise
Of the circled sky around us
And the leathered earth below.
A rock, as in REM sleep,
Boldly swims the naked night
And I dream of you with eagle's lust
And turn with taloned hope –
My seat belt keeping me away
And all my rarified thoughts at bay.
You sleep
Like valleyed clouds at dawn
Unwarmed and yet at rest –
Your doe-like eyes
Pavillioned with velvet shutters
And secure against the world –
While all around us
Life goes on
Suspended by invention
And our fear of open skies.

House Fire

Have you ever smelled a house fire?
No! I mean, really smelled it
Like a perfumer smells lavender or thyme?
Smelled it in the acrid smoke
Or in the damp ash of fire done?
Smelled it at your own place –
Your mound of emberless dreams.
Or maybe at another's
As you hold their sooty hands and cry.

You can't mistake it for a campfire
Or a holiday hearth,
Or incense in some pretty dish –
These wishes gone in flame.

This smoke is painful –
Stings the eyes and makes you weep,
But not enough
To save the things you loved –
The things, perhaps,
That give this smoke
Its singular and indelible smell.
The scent of mortality and the lifelessness of ash.
A scent we dread to smell again –
Anywhere
But especially in our soul.

Illumination

Knowledge is like wood or wax –
Some carve and shape it
And in aesthetic fervor
Worship its resulting form –
Celebrate the artist
Who is really
Only a manipulator of the Truth –
A craftsman unaware of the Divine potential
In every fallen scrap.

Charmed ahead, like all the rest,
They gaze amazed at what they've made.
The "I" in eye
Is blinded by their craft
Until beholders drift bewildered
Through the numened night's display
Quite unaware there's more within
The din of adulation holds at bay.

True blessing only comes within the flame
Where alchemy Divinely sublimates the soul –
Where wood and wax are changed by light –
Where oaken hearts are opened by the fire;
And warming wax is drawn to supplication's deliquescent wick.
The dream is entered as we melt into the bright mélange;
Able there to truly see,
And seeing Being,
Dissolve into Your all-consuming love
And shine!

Love Poem

The pen is my prison and the page the yard I walk,
Longing for the freedom just beyond the fencing words
That isolate me in the confines of vocabulary and
The limits explanation puts upon the poem.
If I could write in soulful ink no darker than the harvest moon
On pages of imagination lined with nothing but
    unbounded grace,
Perhaps this bird could set his wings
Upon the uncaught ether of another way
And rise on eddies known, but nameless,
To the cloudless skies of worlds beyond my troubled thoughts
To perch, unfooted, like the morning light on rising blooms.
And there, as vapors slip to artless air I need to breathe,
To utter just a sigh of truth, like love's recall,
Then fall exhausted on the page in some semantic siege,
Knowing still, the joy of flight and the freedom tasted in
    the undone dew –
With you, still wet upon my lips.

Purgatory

What if I could sense again my teenage heart –
Know first – love and vibrant, responsive flesh.
Ears where wind still whispered in the distant trees
And eyes that saw soft smiles from far away;
Well-oiled hinges and limber limbs,
Like saplings in summer storms
Whose tear-wet leaves still fight for life
And bud to bring the bee's delight;
A time when time was just an unused clock
And night, the comma in a cascade of ideas,
Vetted in the morning by undaunted innocence
And a solar zest to taste the light.

I saw this all in dusky days.
I must be careful
Or I'll find myself wishing for heaven
All over again.

The Plow

I remember plowing on the farm –
The corners were the hardest with one arm.
But dad had taught me, with his trust,
To spin the wheel and then to thrust
Hydraulics up and down again with speed
And showed me with each conquered weed
That life is like a field to spade
Whose working yields a silvered blade
Reflecting all around its light
And giving peaceful sleep at night.

And now I live in concrete fields
Where sidewalk cracks grow meager yields
Of weeds or grass which seem sublimely
In a place unkempt, untimely,
Trying boldly for the sky –
  Unheralded by each passerby.

But I look down with fonder gaze
Remembering those farming days
Where furrows turned to polish steel
And then a strange communion feel
With weeds who've conquered man-made stone
And beat the odds and fully grown,
And see myself as plow and ground
And wonder at the things I've found
And where I've come from, then till now,
And know it started on that plow.

The Wave

First but a gleam, far, far away,
Even and shiny, and void of its spray;
Silver it slithers in towards the shore –
Now somewhat nearer, and gathering more –
Building and climbing and summoning strength,
Brewing up power and boiling its length;
Deepening curve and sharpening curl,
Grasping and gulping the sea with a swirl
Cupping its tonnage, its length and its height,
And smashing the shoreline with cascades of white;
Tossing its treasure of sapphire spray,
Blasting up brilliant! then slipping away . . .

Time

Time is the great vast wall
That keeps now
From then and when –
Abyss of our everything,
Shadow of our nothingness.
The keeper of us all.

John Herndon

John Herndon teaches writing and literature at Austin Community College, where he also serves as the associate director of the Balcones Center for Creative Writing. Among his books of poetry are *Survival Notes*, *Poems from Undertown*, *Road Trip Through the Four Spheres*, *Proof that the World is Real* and *Mapping the Debris Field*. His poems, essays and reviews have been widely published. He studied literature, philosophy, the classics and modern languages at the University of Texas. Herndon has worked as a reporter and critic for the *Austin American-Statesmen*, producer and host for KJFK-FM and KUT-FM, and host of the *Poetry Journal* television series.

Laurel Ash Olmos
(1917 - 1989)

I wandered out one morning
lonely as a cloud, no   alone
alone in blessed solitude

by the river gathered shells for dye
free and easy   off the path
into the deep woods, against park rules
hunting purple coneflower, arnica, mullein
for scrapes and bruises, coughs and colds

all these years the only moment to myself
my only chance and even so
only in the name of doing for others

     When the clouds set down,
     these woods feel deeply

         Mother and grandmother, she walked
         with her head bent, stopped, stooped, dropped
         on hands and knees feeling beneath needles
         strewn on the forest floor, stroking
         under fat oak leaves, caressing the little
                  longspike silver bluestem
         probing between pebbles
            acorns and pine cones

Follow your nose smack into the clear
blue fluted petals and hairy leaves

of vivacious, metaphysical chicory
say Yes! to the universe

                              oh well

if you don't find what you're looking for
you take what you can find
bargain-hunter-gatherer's wisdom

we can eat these leaves and flowers in a salad
bury autumn roots in sandy compost and water
hide them in the closet and sprout chicons,
        baby heads sautéed in butter
as Belgian endive – delicious!

the little ones will sure enjoy seeing
blue flowers turn red set in an ant bed
        action of formic acid

        ah ha! sweet woodruff
steeped in a bottle of Liebfraumilch
and two drams of Cognac will
make a man merry and a woman carefree

my Rick and me frisky as teens

                She rose, inhaling deep the potpourri
                smoothing her hair with one hand

                sun broke fallstreaks of maidenhair
                ephemera never touched the ground
                rainbow bridged   earth and sky
                and a halo of spectral light encircled her

                four cardinals made the sign of the cross
                over her head

                                        she could not stop
                        but her feet felt rooted to the spot

This can't be it

        The precise moment of beginning and ending
        when the bright glories came and went
                impossible to determine

                The zenith broadcast seeds of brilliant blue
                spreading rays like an eight-spoked wheel
                above a fearful, dirty gray

                high in the east blazed dazzling white
                sympathy that filled her with love
                though the horizon sulked with angry smoke

                the south glowed saffron and gold
                warmth and wisdom above
                the jaundiced hue produced by
                humans with their little minds

                fantastic flames soared in the west
                like mercy promised to all
                while below seeped bloody rust
                clotted with narrow greed

                mounting the north the infinite
                shades of living chlorophyll
                descended to the sick verdigris
                of burning copper or rotten bronze
                patina eaten with acid rain

Away, away, thou light-winged hermit thrush
ethereal flute enwinding shadowy cedars
I cannot see what flowers are at my feet

far away, fly and fade
into the pure, clear colors of the sky
void and cloudless as naked intellect
without center or circumference

but wolfsbane, yewberry, nightshade
        la belladonna senza grazie
perplex and retard the most diaphanous flight

She felt nothing   nothing

        but pressure, as if she were sinking
        into a small tarn rimmed with pines

        settling she saw the pool
        dish, cup, bowl, arch and vault
        under the mounting weight of water
        but the powerful, suffocating depth
        perfectly balanced the pressure within
        swelling to burst her skin, she prayed

Please, please, so help me
        this can't be it!
I'll give everything I've got,
make a pilgrimage, or else!
Else what? Abjure faith, abandon hope
sell myself and take the money with me!

The lake dried up, and she sank down
stuck in the cold mud
pathetic old breasts flat and fallen
veins choked hard, bloody womb
turned inside out

How'd I ever let myself get so fat?

But that is nothing   nothing now
shed that heaviness, I can fly, I can fly
with the speed of thought anywhere I think of

Denali, great one, water made stone

Tahoma, the mountain that was god

debris of sacred groves, Pacific
                waves translucent green

from the Range of Light to the Black Hills
        with a single wing-beat
stormy Katahdin to Tlaloc, licker of toads

overlapping centers and boundaries

desecrated Doko'o'slid scarred with ski-trails
Tso Dzil poisoned with uranium tailings

at the foot of Malintzi eat the flesh of god

Llullaillaco overlooking Atacama
place of sacrifice above 22,000 feet

Chomolongma, Goddess of the Wind

Kailas, manifestation of invisible Meru
rising in isolate splendor above the Lake of the Mind

I fly to Meru, fly through the mountain
top to bottom   side to side   equally easy

like one who left home in her youth
and forgot the way back to her birthplace
I set off for home tomorrow
                    and got there yesterday

I love my children, like any mother
          but I need my privacy, too
kids, with kids of their own, but still kids

Oh Rickie, I've never seen you cry
why won't you say something
I'll never speak to you again!

This can't be it!

                    An intermittent rain of yellow leaves
                    wafted into drifts, smoldered with wet heat
                              like fresh-heaped compost
                    till the moisture steamed away

                    she wandered the paths of inaction
                    in misty light not cast by moon or stars
                    but seeming to emanate
                    from the rocks, trees, streams, the very air

                         katabatic wind
                    churning tygers in the snow
                    burning snake-eyes in the rain

she fled through crumbling mountains
from somewhere came a roaring
fire, seas overflowing, spring wind

and the way was cut off in three directions
cliffs of limestone, slate, red granite
the way out, a way that is not a way
beyond yet another beyond
colorless   abandoned

pitiful thing, worthless old woman
faded and tattered finery draped on dry sticks
a bloated bag full of shit and entrails

no one to sit by her side and chant
except the indifferent cicada, worrisome raccoon

coyote feasted on guts
crow pecked eyes
vulture tore sensitive nipples

That's no part of me or mine
what's needed is a vermifuge
raw carrots and fresh garlic, cayenne of course
lemon water and pumpkin seeds
tansy seeds and lots of thyme
no more than a sprig of wormwood
in a tonic wine a little at a time

Anabatic wind
forced into a crack in the stone
hard enough to forge a diamond

Be a little lady, they said
I caught the eyes of little boys
they chased me, I hated them

then my blood flowed from
a wound that would never heal

a wound in the middle of my being

one I let catch me, favored
lips, words and kisses, caresses

　　　then I hated him
hated my swollen body
breasts full and tender
Daddy yelled and Mama cried
and I screamed

oh! little baby gone before
gone before we hardly knew

how will I know you when we meet again?
　　　　　I'd know you anywhere

Mama and Daddy, I can't remember your faces
how will I know you?
　　　oh, how could we forget?

Don't blame me, it's not my fault
I'm just a woman, weaker vessel
a man's world, let go

met another, steady fellow
not brilliant, or beautiful, but kind
fond of his drink at the end of a long, hard day

he deserved it, he earned it
little enough to ask for a lifetime
of degrading jobs, work without meaning
what fields we are called to labor in

took me to wife, soon mother
Lizbeth, Peter, Annie, Sissie
never got a proper name
no love like the love of your children

they can be such a pain
can't blame him, the stress!
can't blame me, oh sure
he yelled, he cussed, what man doesn't?

he only wanted to be a good
disciplinarian like his daddy

when I put myself between the father
and children, I was scared
too late, little Sissie, too late

what could I do? a woman alone
with five, four, three, sleep, shriek, struggle
no escape, down on your knees

what work, for a woman
work and worker despised
lower than the lowliest
made my need their need

and if I left my kids to others
I had to feed them, didn't I?
clothe them, put them through school

how many hours passed
picking up and putting up
washing dishes, dirty laundry
folding clothes and putting them away
days and days peeling potatoes and onions
slicing ham, slapping together sandwiches
cooking big pots of beans and stew
then doing the dishes again
weeks on end wandering miles and miles
through markets, wiping faces and bottoms
years drying runny noses
with catnip, eyebright, elecampane
lifting gloomy moods with cloves
calming spirits with chamomile
rosemary for memory and clear thinking
generations waiting for the kettle to boil
steeping fennel and angelica
to ease the monthly cramp and flow
soothing nipples with carrot, comfrey, yarrow
borage and dill, fenugreek for nursing
sage to dry up milk at weaning time
and for breast infections
continuous packs of strong peach tea
ten thousand mornings first one up
down on my knees, still in my nightdress
blowing the fire aflame
                              in these latitudes
more for companionship and cheer than warmth

I worked so long and hard
I hardly knew what I lost
till I found my 'Rique, so good to me
Enrique, I love you, goodbye

The flame leapt like a trout out of water
mixing clouds and fire and air
a mirror where she saw a twisted red
madrone, ancient, many-breasted

living wood entwined the long dead
leaves like a hundred lips spoke
incomprehensible prophesy

her good angel and bad angel
counted black and white stones
bailiff and executioner escorted the angry judge

my neighbor's pot refused to boil, she explained
the water ran out through a hole
but I returned it in good shape
it was punctured when I borrowed it
and I never borrowed it in the first place

The judge smiled as his hit men
tied me to a tree
trunk of twisted serpents
fruits the head of women
set my feet in the fire
                    for my own good

I screamed till my jaw would crack
a crack where the wind blows
          drowning my cries

When the great cloud belches
mountain forests lash and sway
huge firs 100 spans around
with noses, mouths, ears
cups, mortars, jugs

roar like waves, whistle like arrows
screech, gasp, cry, wail, moan, howl

the music of what is

beneath the boulder, at length
passage into the mountain

warm and dark and still
the narrow fissure opened
a chamber where she could stand

and the heat steamed her dry
a dry heat, and a light far
behind, below, above, beyond

shadow light

a wall of fossiliferous stone
the story of all her days

Born beneath a rock
conceived by semen in sea-foam
Mother died in childbirth
I midwived my twin

I loved him like my own son
he was there to protect me, he said

Endowed with a magical alphabet
knowledge of the secret name
sacred to the goddess
and from my trunk the gods emerged
as the branches around a tree

I veiled my naked mystery with a thousand leaves
serpents coiled my limbs, and my brother
found his desire in my writhing

delighted in woods and wilds
by the river gathered many a shell
many a pretty flower and medicinal weed

hair carelessly caught by a single pink ribbon

like fire in dry grass on a mountain slope
my twin pursued me where I fled
among the enchanted trees
the virgin laurel, and the loyal elm

pricked by diverse arrows, gold and lead
we ran swift as hope and fear
I called my heavenly father's name
and lost my twin where I left the trail

but in my father's kingdom a rape
conceived is the same as committed

in the woods beyond the four directions
                    found my father

drunk on the unmixed wine, he said
the blush on your cheek like foxglove flowers
would make a priest forget his vows

at the foot of the oak he forced me

                    Gnarled roots barked her shins
                    hard wood spread her legs

                              soft breast grew hard

leaves and vines twined in her hair
her mother, proper helpmeet, held her
shoulders to the dirt
                              a misbegotten act

her cries went unanswered
listening elders bent their heads
treetop covered her face, concealed her lips
she tore her hair and plucked out leaves

in hot sun tears hardened
                              to amber and myrrh

curled mid the bole of a chestnut tree
she waited her time

grief-stricken nighthawks wheeled about her crown

the trunk bellied and bulged, cracked and groaned
until the delicate lightning split the tree
and she was born again, full grown

wrapped her tears in a sycamore leaf
and hid them under a stone

she walked like the night
past rivers and deserts and coasts
mountains shaggy with hemlock

into a wide plain where she found
the tree where her father hanged himself
first slashing the abusive member

where blood and sperm dripped
flame acanthus flourished

giant cypress six could not embrace
vine grew up and snaked
a limb above her head
where hung a skull

which is the way? she said
come closer, open your hand
so I can see, said the skull

she complied
          and the dry bone spit in her palm

she looked in her hand, it was dry
but something was moving in her belly

journeyed a year and a day
till she came to the foretold place
gave birth to feathers and fur
briars and yaupon, thickets
of magnolia and pine
all wet and glistening in the sun

with reverence she entered the sacred grove
tall patriarchs and matriarchs standing apart
holding open space with long limbs

elysian light fell in rays and pools

healthy community
young and mature and aged
all growing and living and dying together

and some, really old,
abandoned all sense of propriety
and threw their limbs in extravagant gestures

there she was welcome
held glad talk with mother and father
baby and little Sissie and all
who loved her unconditionally

Stay with me and hold me in the day

All smiles, they withdrew

What has happened, I accept
and what has not, that too I accept

When she fell, no human ear
was near, but she made a thunderous crash

the noise inherent in things

as long as she stood upright on the earth
that long till she returned completely

deep languor lay on her limbs
embroidery of white fungus threads
aerobic cooking with enzymes
prokaryotic ancestral mass
soft monerans' warm embrace

Pitchy heartwood and dry branches
burned by booted, bearded pilgrims
exhausted under heavy packs
fuel for cooking, warmth and light
so they could rest awhile and revive
their spirits, I gave willingly, lovingly

A living moving
system of chaos
flame enfolded her

releasing pent-up sunlight
dissolved the boundaries between this and that

redeemed from rot
the illusion of self

dissociate atoms rose on warm air

spread through a cubic mile of sky
where myriad seeds and spiders
        drift like plankton
bathed by ephemeral virga

So this is it!

Cast no reflection
blow out the flame
of worry and desire

when you can forget what can be forgotten
and forget what cannot be forgotten
that can be called forgetting

where opposites are no longer opposed
is the hinge of the way

whatever you desire will come to pass
        desire nothing
egg, womb or virgin birth

when men and women couple
conceive no jealousy or hate
for mother or father
choose enlightened parents

plant a seedling in the corpse's mouth
there springs the tree of mercy

from a long, subtle hummock
the last trace of a ghost
sprout vigorous young ones

work worth doing

save all sentient beings
loosen the soil and hold it firm
capture carbon, liberate oxygen

furnish house and home
for springtail, pill bug, millipede
field mouse and screech owl
beetle and woodpecker

nurture mushrooms
in humus culture
nematodes thin as hair, thick as hair
millions to the handful

ever youthful, ever dying
ecstatic equilibrium

hold heaven and earth together
and keep them apart

Contributors

Editor **Robert Bonazzi** directed the independent literary imprint Latitudes Press from 1966 to 2000, producing over 100 titles. He joined Wings Press in 2003, on a *pro bono* basis, to continue a long literary collaboration with publisher Bryce Milligan, an old friend and fellow-poet. Bonazzi has published five books of poetry, most recently *Maestro of Solitude*, and the critically acclaimed *Man in the Mirror: John Howard Griffin and the Story of Black Like Me*. He writes a column on poetry, "Poetic Diversity," for the *San Antonio Express-News*.

Cover artist **Andrea Belag's** large-format art book, *Andrea Belag*, contains 30 works in color, plus commentary and an interview. It was jointly published by Galerie Heinz Holtmann (Köln) and the Bill Maynes Gallery (New York). Belag had two one-person shows in 2007: *Vienna Blue* at the Philadelphia Museum of Jewish Art and *New Paintings* at the Mike Weiss Gallery in New York. Several paintings by Belag that have graced the covers of Wings Press books.

Acknowledgments

Several of Nancy Kenney Connolly's poems are reprinted from *Mobius, The Glass Eye, Softblow, The Pedestal Magazine, Main Street Rag, DiVerseCity, Red Owl* and *Frost Place Anthology*. Three of Del Marie Rogers's poems were published in *The Texas Observer* and *Samsara*. Most of the poems by Tony Zurlo have appeared in *Long Story Short, Snow Monkey, New Texas, AIAP (All Info About Poetry), Peace Corps Writers, The Sunday Suitor Poetry Journal, The Word* and *DiVerseCity*. Assef Al-Jundi's "Holy Landers" was first published in *The Texas Observer*. Laura Quinn Guidry's "Alone" was published in *Concho River Review*. Their poems are reprinted here with the permission of these publications, and all previously unpublished poems appear in this anthology with the permission of the poets.

List of Titles

Wings Press was founded in 1975 by Joanie Whitebird and Joseph F. Lomax, both deceased, as "an informal association of artists and cultural mythologists dedicated to the preservation of the literature of the nation of Texas." Publisher, editor and designer since 1995, Bryce Milligan is honored to carry on and expand that mission to include the finest in American writing – meaning all of the Americas, without commercial considerations clouding the choice to publish or not to publish.

Wings Press attempts to produce multicultural books, chapbooks, CDs, DVDs and broadsides that we hope enlighten the human spirit and enliven the mind. Everyone ever associated with Wings has been or is a writer, and we know well that writing is a transformational art form capable of changing the world, primarily by allowing us to glimpse something of each other's souls. Good writing is innovative, insightful, and interesting. But most of all it is honest.

Likewise, Wings Press is committed to treating the planet itself as a partner. Thus the press uses as much recycled material as possible, from the paper on which the books are printed to the boxes in which they are shipped.

Associate editor Robert Bonazzi is also an old hand in the small press world. Bonazzi was the editor and publisher of Latitudes Press (1966-2000). Bonazzi and Milligan share a commitment to independent publishing and have collaborated on numerous projects over the past 25 years.

As Robert Dana wrote in *Against the Grain,* "Small press publishing is personal publishing. In essence, it's a matter of personal vision, personal taste and courage, and personal friendships." Welcome to our world.

WINGS PRESS

Colophon

This first edition of *In These Latitudes: Ten
Contemporary Poets*, edited by Robert Bonazzi,
has been printed on 70 pound paper containing
50 percent recycled fiber. Titles have been set in
Papyrus type, the text is in Adobe Caslon type.
All Wings Press books are designed and
produced by Bryce Milligan.

On-line catalogue and ordering
available at
www.wingspress.com

Wings Press titles are distributed
to the trade by the
Independent Publishers Group
www.ipgbook.com